The Act of Meditation

The Act of Meditation

*by Robert R. Leichtman, M.D.
& Carl Japikse*

ENTHEA PRESS
Atlanta, Georgia & Columbus, Ohio

THE ACT OF MEDITATION
Copyright © 1988 by Light

All Rights Reserved. No part of this book may be used or reproduced in any manner without written permission, except in the case of brief quotations embodied in articles and reviews. Printed in the United States of America. Direct inquiries to Enthea Press, 289 S. Main Street, Alpharetta, GA 30201.

ISBN 0-89804-830-3

Introduction

This essay, *The Act of Meditation,* was first published as part of a set of 30 essays written by Robert R. Leichtman, M.D. and Carl Japikse on *The Life of Spirit.* It can also be found in Volume III of that series.

It has been selected to be reprinted in this special gift edition because it is the clearest concise description in print of the use of meditation as a key exercise in the life of spirit. It can be thought of as a prologue to the authors' far more comprehensive work on the topic, *Active Meditation: The Western Tradition.*

For information about ordering other essays by Dr. Leichtman and Mr. Japikse, please turn to page 96.

The Presence of Spirit

8

In learning to use the tools of spirit, we must realize that these are special tools, not at all like the kind of tool we buy at a discount house, use for a few years, then discard, once it is worn out. The tools of spirit actually grow with use and become more powerful; the more adept we become at using any one of them, the more its usefulness to us expands and deepens. In the early stages of aspiration, for example, our major focus is on discovering spirit and learning to use it in simple ways for the benefit of the personality. As a result, we are likely to view the tools of spirit in this light, seeing prayer as a means of soliciting what we want from the soul, meditation as a means of finding out about our inner senses, and worship as a highly personal act of devotion. As aspiration ripens into the spiritual life, however, our emphasis shifts. Gradually, we move away from our adolescent fascination with what spirit can do for us and begin to understand spirit for what it is—the noble essence of our life. We become more interested in learning what spirit is seeking to accomplish through our life, and we dedicate our mind, heart, and physical energies to serving the purposes of spirit. As this shift occurs, we also begin using the tools of spirit in a new way, with a healthier appreciation for their real power and purpose. We start using them as a means for *serving* and *expressing* spirit in the fabric of our daily life—using prayer to bless, cleanse, and heal; confession to activate our spiritual design; meditation to integrate spirit with the personality, and so on.

This just makes sense. Any effective tool can be used in a variety of ways, from the childish to the enlightened. Television, for example, can be a marvelous medium enriching our life by educating us about other cultures, informing us about current events, entertaining us with great drama, music, and art, and stimulating our mind in many diverse ways. Far too often, however, we use television only as a means of escape—to make a dull life seem less dull, to relieve our boredom by soaking up a few empty hours, or to keep the kids occupied for awhile. Obviously, mature and intelligent people use television in ways that enrich their lives—while entertaining them. But those who view television only as a means of escape will tune into any kind of program, regardless of how crude or trivial it might be.

And herein lies a problem—a problem which carries over into our use of the tools of spirit as well. The person who watches television indiscriminately exposes himself or herself to a lot of programming which is little more than trash—soap operas glorifying selfishness, greed, and malice; music which stimulates our lowest instincts and sensations; and prime time dramas reveling in violence, neurotic behavior, and simplistic sentiments. Addiction to this kind of stimulation can rob the individual of initiative, making him a creation of television. The tool ends up dominating its user, instead of being used skillfully and wisely to enrich life.

The tools of spirit have been created by spirit to serve its purposes and designs. As such, each tool has tremendous power to enrich our life—when properly used. But like television, the tools of spirit can be misused—to entertain those who dream of a spiritual life even though they have no real interest in living one, to pursue selfish goals, or to provide the pleasant illusion that we are in touch with spirit and responsive to it, even though we are only in touch with our feelings. And when the tools of spirit are misused in this way, we run the risk of actually becoming alienated from the life of spirit, addicted to our misuse and unable to see how we are limiting ourself.

Meditation in particular is prone to these nonspiritual and even destructive uses. Properly used, meditation is a most remarkable tool, enabling us to transcend our ordinary states of awareness and enter into the realm of spirit. From this higher level of activity, we can then contact divine forces directly, fill our consciousness with them, and focus them in specific and creative ways into the lower levels of our self-expression for the purpose of healing, transforming, enriching, and renewing.

And yet, just as television is not always used to educate, inform, discover, and enrich, meditation, too, is not always used according to its spiritual design. It is often used just to entertain ourself—or to make the life of the personality easier in some way.

There is certainly a place in everyone's life for entertainment and making the life of the personality easier—but we do not need a tool of spirit to do these things. And using a tool of spirit in this way can generate great problems for us, if we are interested in treading the spiritual path.

The primary ways that "meditation" is improperly used as a tool of the personality, rather than a tool of spirit, include:

Simple relaxation. Just as the lowest level of programming on television is often the most appealing to the average viewer, so also the simplest activities involved in entering a meditative state are often confused for meditation itself. Especially in recent years, meditation has been widely touted as a relaxation exercise and a means for escaping stress. It is true that it is necessary to relax the body and our tense focus of thought and feeling before we can meditate, but it is a major error to confuse relaxation with meditation. Nor is very much relaxation even conducive to good meditation; those who believe that a deep, trance-like state is a sign of profound meditation are off the mark. Excessive relaxation produces a dreamy state more closely resembling sleep than expanded alertness, and can induce a dissociated state of consciousness which is the direct opposite of what a good meditative level of awareness should be!

Relaxation has its obvious benefits, but those who need to relax ought to take a nap or soak in a tub. Meditation is meant to be an enlightening and enriching experience, producing transformation.

Cheap psychic thrills. The purpose of meditation is to lift our awareness out of its limited focus in the personality, so it can identify with spirit and interact with divine qualities. It must be understood, however, that there are many levels of consciousness—not just physical and spiritual. In fact, as we withdraw from our physical level of alertness, the first level we will encounter will be the emotional or astral plane, not the spiritual. To reach the level of the soul, we cannot stop at this level—this would be tantamount to being in touch only with our feelings! We must continue to lift our awareness, through the astral, even through the lower levels of the mental plane, until we truly identify with the soul and the abstract, divine forces of the higher mental plane.

Unfortunately, just as many television viewers would rather watch a game show than a thoughtful discussion of world issues, many would-be meditators are more interested in the voices and visions of the astral plane than they are in contacting the true force of spirit. Astral awareness produces a whole host of psychic sensations, and these impressions are often so fascinating and new that they are invariably mistaken as signs of significant breakthrough into the "highest" realm of spirit. Indeed, in the Spiritualist tradition, the term "spiritual" is used to refer to the astral plane, which is an utter absurdity.

In meditating, we must take care not to be distracted by the subjective sensations, sounds, and images of the astral plane. Most of these are simple projections from our own subconscious, which, after all, knows better than anyone which cheap thrills turn us on. If we become absorbed in these pictures, symbols, and feelings, we will quickly become trapped in our own self-deception. The purpose of meditating will be defeated.

Chanting and panting. True meditation occurs at abstract levels of consciousness—at the realm of spirit. It is difficult for the beginning meditator to understand the dynamics of meditation at these levels, however, and so various practices have been developed over the centuries to help students become more aware of and responsive to these inner happenings. The soul's ability to sound keynotes in consciousness, for example, was set forth as a science of sound or the use of mantras. The soul's capacity to inspire us and infuse our life with the force of spiritual qualities was presented as the science of breathing. Other practices, such as the visualization of symbols and the use of physical postures, also evolved. Unfortunately, as the years progressed and the traditions became established, the inner realities they were intended to portray became forgotten. Teachers and students alike began to regard these traditions *as vital parts of the meditative exercise,* not as minor adjuncts which help the beginning student focus his or her attention.

There is great charm to these practices, because it is relatively easy to chant and pant—to sound a mantra or focus on our breath. It requires no commitment to spirit, no dedication to making changes in our thoughts, attitudes, or lifestyle—not even any interest in discovering our spiritual self. These practices are therefore quite appealing to those who wish for spiritual progress in the easiest, most effortless way. After all, it is far easier to keep our spine straight than it is to straighten out messy, selfish emotions. It is far easier to regulate our breath than it is to regulate ambivalent and conflicting thoughts and attitudes. It is far easier to sound a mantra than it is to respond to spirit and serve its plan.

Many of these practices are doubly appealing because they come to us from exotic, ancient, and foreign traditions. For some reason, many people are willing to believe in almost anything that has been practiced by generation after generation of Hindus—or better yet, Tibetans. And so they practice them, too, as a form of meditation, even though all this huffing and puffing, chanting and panting does not lead to any discernible improvement in character, mental clarity, or purification and healing of the emotions, let alone contact with spirit.

Of course, the use of these practices

does produce some alteration of consciousness, which is why people keep using them. But not all altered states of consciousness are desirable ones. In most cases, the use of mantras, breathing exercises, and Hatha Yoga asanas leads to a state of "spiritual boredom" in which our active consciousness is numbed. This anesthetizes us to the trauma, irritation, and agitation of daily life—but does not lead to any wholesome or creative enrichment of character. In fact, it often leaves the "meditator" vulnerable to psychic manipulation and domination from lower astral forces and entities.

Hypnosis and guided imagery. The growing use of hypnosis and guided imagery to help people make changes at subconscious levels has further clouded the issue of what is meditation, what is not. Both hypnosis and guided imagery can be valuable tools when properly used by knowledgeable people—but they should not be confused for meditation. Nor should meditation be adapted to serve the purposes of hypnosis or guided imagery. Unfortunately, many of those who use hypnosis and guided imagery do not understand what meditation is and how it differs from these and other practices, and carelessly lump them all together as one.

Some of the techniques of hypnosis and guided imagery do superficially resemble some of the more simplistic techniques of effective meditation, and even produce some of the same results—changes in moods, memories, attention, motivation, and habits. But these are the incidentals of meditation. The true purpose of meditation is to expand our awareness and enrich the quality of consciousness, by contacting the life of spirit—and neither hypnosis nor guided imagery makes this contact. The visualizations of guided imagery have only the power of the imagination behind them. The suggestions of self-hypnosis have only the power of the personality behind them. But the symbols, archetypal patterns, and qualities contacted in meditation have the power of spirit behind them.

When meditation is properly practiced, it is guided by the wisdom of spirit—not by images or hypnotic suggestions. The danger of confusing self-hypnosis and the use of visualizations for meditation is that many people will stagnate at the level of their imagination. Instead of contacting spirit, they will use meditative techniques only to manipulate images or implant suggestions in the subconscious. This robs meditation of its true potential.

As a way to build cults. There are always charismatic opportunists who are eager to build a power base for their own self-aggrandizement. Most of these people are attracted either to politics or religion. Those who go into religion find it difficult to gain much attention in established faiths, so they start a cult. And in order to attract people to their cult, they have to offer something which looks like a technique for spiritual growth. So they put together a package of hypnotic exercises, add such mystical trappings as deep breathing, the repetition of mantras, and group movements, and then label it "meditation." But the purpose of this "meditation" is not to promote contact with spirit; on the contrary, it is carefully designed to promote passiveness and inner numbness, so the members of the cult can be deftly brainwashed by the leader.

This perversion of meditation is far more common than most people realize or are willing to admit. There is a strong tendency among men and women of goodwill to assume that everyone who says he or she is on the spiritual path actually is; we forget all too easily that many of the people who tread the path the most conspicuously are doing so only to gain influence over the ones who tread it with devotion and genuine aspiration. We also fail to realize that those who extol the virtues of passive meditation—in particular, Zen and those Eastern traditions which emphasize guru worship—often have no contact whatsoever with the higher self. Their great accomplishment is their mastery of the ancient techniques of brainwashing and mind control.

Just because something is labeled "meditation" and used by thousands of "satisfied customers" is no guarantee that it will be effective—or that it is, indeed, meditation. Only those practices which help us rise out of our personal focus, identify with spirit, and learn to work consciously and skillfully with divine force ought to be called meditation. *If we are going to use meditation as a tool of spirit, we had better learn to distinguish between those meditative practices which serve the life of spirit and those which serve only the personality, embracing the former and rejecting the latter.* And we had better learn that just calling something spiritual does not in any way make it spiritual.

After all, a person who watches arts and cultural programs on television and one who watches soap operas and game shows can both be said to be "watching television," yet the experiences are almost completely unrelated. Just so, a person who identifies with spirit, absorbs its qualities, and focuses them into his conscious awareness and one who sounds a mantra or calms himself down with a simple relaxation exercise may both refer to their activities as "meditation," yet there is no similarity between them at all.

Real meditation is a way of coming to know the presence of spirit—not in theory, not in pretty images, not as a blind belief, not as an intellectual concept, not through a guru, and not as something vague and undefinable, but as a direct and intimate experience of its divine love, wisdom, will, joy, and peace. These experiences may not be flashy or overwhelming—if they are, they are probably just of the astral plane—but they are specific and repeatable. They are specific because in real meditation the emphasis is put not on "blissing out" but on learning to harness and use the powers of spirit to enrich our awareness and nurture our own expression of love, wisdom, will, joy, and peace. And they are repeatable because the whole thrust of real meditation is to build skills in using this tool of spirit.

While dilettantes lust for powerful and dramatic flashes of light, surges of power, and intense sensations during meditation, the genuine presence of spirit is more commonly discovered in our own quiet development of greater compassion toward the present, greater tolerance toward our past, new insight into the future, and a greater sense of peace and stability about who we are and the events of our life. The experience of harnessing and focusing these qualities in our life is worth more than all we could possibly read about them, or about spirit, in a year.

In genuine meditation, we contact divine life—"the power which can make all things new." This is the power of spirit; it is greater than any of the talents, skills, and capacities of the personality. As such, it is a tremendous source for transformation and growth within us—and this is precisely why a conscious interaction with spirit is so important. Just going numb in the head will not produce these transformations; something more is required.

How do we know when we have contacted spirit? True meditative contact with spirit will set in motion three definite changes in consciousness. It will:

Expand our awareness. The life of the personality is defined by its finiteness—by its limited capacity to love, understand, experience, and act. We can always annex new ideas, feelings, experiences, and philosophies to the personality—through education, travel, and reflection—but this simply makes our storehouse of knowledge and feelings a little more crowded. It does not expand our awareness. As we contact the life of spirit, however, and meditatively interact with its patterns, qualities, and forces, our consciousness actually grows. It does not expand in the sense of a balloon being blown up, but in the sense of increasing our capacity to comprehend our potential, love life, and express ourself creatively. In this way, new wisdom, love, and will enter our awareness, quickening the good and noble elements within us and enabling them to expand.

Our awareness of divine wisdom expands as we begin viewing life as spirit views it, increasing our ability to make sense of ideas and work more creatively.

Our awareness of divine love expands as we tap the impersonal yet benevolent compassion of spirit toward all things, increasing our capacity to treat others and the events of life with greater goodwill, tolerance, and forgiveness.

Our awareness of divine will expands as we discover the force of spiritual direction which has guided us through life, the presence of divine purpose overshadowing our daily work, and the power of spirit, increasing our courage and perseverance.

Our awareness of the life of spirit expands as we learn to recognize and respond to the indwelling presence of God everywhere, especially in the midst of our ordinary associations and work, increasing our ability to heal, serve, and help.

Enrich our character. In meditation, the mind is able to fill its awareness with the pure forces of divine compassion, peace, wisdom, harmony, and will and then focus these forces into the matrix of our character, redeeming and transforming our habits, attitudes, convictions, and patterns of behavior. In this way, the act of meditation integrates our inner design for wholeness and perfection with the outer patterns of our character, so that the power of spirit takes root and begins to grow within our personal life. As a result, we are able to use the practice of meditation:

- To do more than just experience the benevolence and peace of God. We can actually use these forces to heal and purify the hurts of the subconscious.
- To do more than just tap new insights. We can actually direct the force of these realizations into our memories and plans, thereby putting our memories in a more wholesome perspective and shaping our plans more effectively.
- To do more than just sense greater meaning and purpose in what we do. We can actually add the *power* of this purpose to our noble aspirations, intentions, and goals, thereby infusing the life of spirit more rapidly into the life of the personality.

There are those who would disagree with this bold statement that meditation can be used to integrate spirit and personality, some contending that such integration is impossible, because the mind is incapable of registering the life of spirit; others holding that it is unnecessary, because spirit works automatically and effortlessly. But these are people who have not updated their understanding of human nature.

When most of the long-standing traditions of meditation were first inaugurated thousands of years ago, few members of humanity had intelligent or well-developed minds. At that time, the mind was incapable of registering the life of spirit. But times have changed, and now large numbers of people do have the necessary mental equipment to register the light of the soul and focus it into the rest of the personality—if they will teach themselves how to do it, through effective meditation.

As for such integrative work being unnecessary, there is no question that holding ourself steady in the light of divine love will have a favorable impact on our consciousness, even if we do nothing specific with it. But if we can focus this light as well as bask in it, we can magnify its impact on our life greatly. For as the personality learns to demonstrate initiative and act wisely, it also enriches its capacity to be used by spirit as an agent for divine wisdom, love, and will. Few things are quite as tragic as the undeveloped spiritual person—the person who loves God with all his heart, but cannot act wisely or dynamically in serving the plan and ideals of God.

Enrich our self-expression. As our character becomes purified and illumined, through meditative contact with spirit, our actual daily behavior and self-expression are enriched. Instead of being mired in the pettiness, triviality, and narrow focus of the personal life, we become more directed by our inner joy, peace, and wisdom. These are not drastic changes; they occur gradually. Almost without realizing it, we begin to approach the challenges of life with greater joy, the duties of our work with renewed creativity, and the limitations we must endure with greater tolerance.

We must always remember that the work of meditation is to lift our consciousness out of its personal focus and attune us, directly and consciously, with the force of spirit. Having done this, spirit does not throw us back into the personality at the end of the meditation to resume living as before. It sends us back with an expanded awareness and an enriched character, and this enables us to act and behave in daily life with greater understanding, peace, forgiveness, joy, and enthusiasm.

One of the great challenges each spiritual aspirant must face is the fundamental question of why we are seeking to grow spiritually. Do we truly aspire to integrate the life of spirit into our daily life, so that we become directed by spirit and adopt the values, goals, and purposes of spirit as our own? Or do we aspire only because we believe that contact with spirit will somehow be to our advantage, and we want this advantage—even though we do not especially want to change our life?

The way in which we meditate will be determined in large measure by how we answer this fundamental question. If we are a spiritual dilettante, interested in spirit only insofar as it can serve us, then we will be most attracted to a meditative regimen which will relax us, soothe us, and help us escape the irritations of life. But as we mature, and become more interested in how we can serve spirit than in how spirit can serve us, we will find such simplistic meditative practices less appealing and less satisfying—because they do not fulfill the design of this great tool of spirit.

The purpose of meditation is much more than simple relaxation, relief from distress, or surrender to God. The tool of meditation gives us a means for communing with spirit and integrating the forces of spirit into our lives, transforming our consciousness, character, and self-expression. Meditation is a means to an end—full rapport with spirit—not the end itself.

As such, the act of meditation is meant to be an intelligent process—not something we embark on blindly, because a teacher tells us it is good for us, but something we pursue maturely, because we understand its value, grasp its principles, and seek to put it to work in our own life.

Fundamental Principles

There is a bewildering number of rituals, techniques, and practices associated with meditation. Some are useful, but many are just experiments which should have been abandoned long ago. Others were helpful when first introduced thousands of years ago, but now have value only as nostalgia. Nonetheless, these traditions are often kept alive by undiscerning aspirants—not because they find them beneficial, but as a demonstration of faith in a teacher who advocates their practice.

A powerful meditative technique or tradition, when practiced properly and on a regular basis, should lead to the gradual but steady transformation of our consciousness and behavior, so that our mind, our heart, and our daily activities are drawn more and more into harmony with the life of spirit. When a meditative technique or tradition does not produce these results, it is probably due to one or more of the following reasons:

There is no specific format which guides the meditator toward genuine contact with spirit. One of the most significant characteristics of consciousness is its structure and design. Spirit does not operate by spontaneous association; it operates by creating specific and precise designs based on the plan of God. It therefore makes sense that the most effective meditation would be that which reflects and embodies the design of spirit for our thinking, feeling, and activity. Yet many of the most popular brands of meditation reject form and structure; they encourage the meditator to empty the mind and become totally passive, so that spirit can take over and guide us spontaneously. Yet this is not the way spirit acts! It is about as intelligent as a housewife throwing away her broom and vacuum cleaner so that the full force of the cleaning power within her can act, unobstructed by any limitations.

The meditator has not made a significant commitment to spiritual change. Just because a person meditates on a regular basis does not mean that this individual has a genuine commitment to the life of spirit. A genuine commitment to the life of spirit implies that we are ready and willing to transform our values, priorities, habits, attitudes, and focus in living so that they serve spirit, not the personality. This means confronting our comfortable acceptance of materialism and replacing it with the light of spirit; it means confronting our selfish habits and values and replacing them with a dedication to serve the plan of God; and it means confronting our ancient habits of self-deception and replacing them with a love for the truth within ourself. This is more than many people want to accept, however, so they adopt a meditative practice which is not so demanding. After all, if they spend all their time mumbling mantras, sending hot flashes up their spine, and hyperventilating, they can avoid the need to examine the quality of their values, attitudes, and behavior—and still believe themselves to be spiritual! Of course, the effectiveness of their meditative work will be almost nil.

There is a poor understanding of the nature and purpose of spirit. Some people believe that since God is One, all we have to do is seek union with this Oneness. We do not have to transform our consciousness, or serve spirit, or bring heaven to earth—in fact, these people claim that spirit has no role on earth except to "rescue" us from our imprisonment here, as though the whole of creation was just a big mistake. As a result, these people assume that the divine design for humanity is to destroy the ego and everything it does. This has a devastating impact on the effectiveness of meditation, however, because it tends to impair and limit consciousness, instead of expand and enrich it. It might be effective "shock treatment" for cases of extreme arrogance and self-centeredness, but it is not a helpful basis for meditation. It undermines the principle of individuality, encourages parasitism, and stunts our sense of enlightened stewardship, which is so very important to the life of spirit.

There is a poor understanding of the role of the personality in the spiritual life. One of the attractions of the spiritual life to some is that it seems to provide an avenue of escape from the drudgery, difficulties, and despair of the personality. These people fail to understand that spirit wants an intelligent, creative, and dynamic personality to act through—not a personality looking for a way out. And yet, there are naturally any number of opportunists who will pander to this thirst for escape, encouraging their followers to surrender to God—or to them—thereby avoiding responsibility for improving themselves. This alone is disastrous to effective meditation, but the damage usually goes even further. Almost always these people teach that the mind is an impediment to spiritual growth and encourage mindlessness, emptiness, and blind belief as spiritual virtues. They put great emphasis on obeying divine will, but do not give their followers the means for discerning it. Obviously, any meditation conducted in this kind of climate will do nothing to strengthen our contact with spirit; it will only strengthen the grip of the teacher on the misplaced loyalties of his or her followers. Intelligent activity is just as important in the work of contacting spirit as in any other serious enterprise. And the most effective meditation will be that which capitalizes on our intelligence—not that which seeks to extinguish it!

Before any meditator adopts a specific tradition or form for meditating, therefore, it is important to look beyond tradition, beyond all of the many techniques and differing approaches to meditation, even beyond religious doctrine, and carefully codify and understand the *principles* of effective meditation. If we do, we will find it relatively easy to make intelligent choices from the smorgasbord of meditative practices; we will also find that whatever meditative format we choose to work in, it will work for us—as long as it is consistent with these fundamental principles. In other words, we will be able to choose the best skills and practices from each meditative tradition and use them productively and intelligently, *because we know why they work!*

The fundamental principles of effective meditation are:

1. The primary focus of meditation must be on the quality of consciousness. This means that the *majority* of the time spent in meditation must be devoted to contacting, exploring, and learning to use the divine qualities of compassion, serenity, wisdom, joy, beauty, and the will—not the use of mantras, breathing exercises, special postures, symbols, or guru worship. Mantras, breathing exercises, and the use of symbols can have their place in the preliminary phases of a meditation, but they must then give way to the more serious activity of shifting our attention to the life of spirit. Obviously, this shift cannot occur if we are focused in our spine, our breath, or a mantra.

It is extremely easy to develop bad habits which prevent us from spending our time in meditation actually focusing on the quality of consciousness. We may start with the vague goal of wanting to "know

God," for example—only to become absorbed in a neverending effort to empty ourself of all thoughts, feelings, and impressions. But a state of emptiness is not the equivalent of a state of knowing God—in fact, it is the direct opposite! Or, at the other extreme, we may become so enchanted by the marvelous visions or pleasant feelings which come into our awareness in our early efforts to meditate that we never probe any deeper into our consciousness. We just use the time of meditation as a trip into the fantasy zones of our own subconscious—which is more than willing to put on spectacular shows to entertain us.

If meditation is going to be used as a tool of spirit, then our primary effort should be to become familiar with the treasures of spirit—our inner capacity for courage, generosity, wisdom, joy, patience, reverence, excellence, harmony, integrity, tolerance, wholeness, and the ability to care. Anything less constitutes a distraction.

2. The goal of meditation is to know

the presence of spirit in both our mind and heart. "Feeling good about God" is better than feeling bad about God, or life, but the act of meditation should take us far beyond good feelings and pleasant sentiments. Having visions of angels and the inner worlds is also nice, but again, there is much, much more we can achieve in meditation! The goal of meditation is to cultivate a new understanding of our relation to God, a new responsiveness to divine patterns and intelligence, and a new capacity to express divine forces in our life. In this way, we not only become aware of the presence of God and learn to love it, but also recreate it in our own mind and heart.

Most meditative traditions fall far short of helping people achieve this goal. All too often, they have settled for just "feeling good about God." This is because they have tended to stress the need for greater faith and love to the exclusion of greater intelligence and strength. The value of faith and love in the spiritual life is unquestioned, but too much of a good thing is still too much! Sentimental longings for divine perfection and a vague, mystical sense of rapport with God may be useful first steps on the spiritual path, but once we have taken the first steps, we are meant to take the subsequent ones as well.

To meditate effectively, we must add intelligent inquiry to our faith, discerning thought to our love, and mature dedication to our devotion. In addition to learning to love God's love, we must learn to understand God's wisdom and will. But this means choosing meditative techniques which exercise the mind as well as our feelings—meditative techniques which teach us the intelligent use of divine love and the loving use of divine intelligence.

3. The practice of meditation is an active skill. The purpose of meditation is to interact with divine force. Anyone who has truly done this knows that divine force is not passive or in any way inactive. All divine forces, including peace, are living energies—vibrant, active, and seeking expression. As we contact these forces and fill our awareness with them, they impel us to initiate activity of our own, first in meditation at a mental level, and later in our daily life at a physical level.

Let it be clearly understood: those who are convinced that meditation consists mainly of emptying our minds and then waiting for God to fill us up simply have not contacted any divine or spiritual forces—just the abundant emptiness within themselves.

This is not to suggest that all kinds of activity are useful to meditation; certainly the tendency of the emotions to worry and the mind to doubt are two notable activities which interfere with effective meditation. But we are meant to mobilize the higher skills and capacities of the mind, emotions, and will to commune with the active light and love of God in meditation. We are meant to:

• Actively cultivate our faith that divine forces are accessible to us and can help us.

• Actively use devotion and aspiration to magnetically link ourself with the love of spirit.

• Actively use the mind to tap divine

wisdom, discern its nature, and apply it to understanding our life.

- Actively use the will to continually dedicate ourself to the supreme authority and direction of spirit.

4. The primary source of our contact with spirit is the indwelling presence of the soul—the immortal essence of life and consciousness within us. Many spiritual aspirants greatly complicate the work of spiritual growth by trying to identify with the universal presence of God—God transcendent—rather than identifying with the presence of God within them—God immanent, the soul. This also renders meditative work rather useless, as it "spaces out" consciousness instead of enriching it. The spaced out state of empty bliss is sometimes mistaken for enlightenment, but it is really a state of spiritual selfishness and indolence. It causes the personality to atrophy, thereby making it impossible for spirit to use it constructively.

Human life is based on the principle of individuality; within each of us is a point of divine awareness which is the indwelling presence of God. Meditation is the act of identifying with this inner point of divinity, the soul, and using it as the central point of our spiritual activity—the integration of the universal with the individual, the divine with the human, the higher with the lower, consciousness with form. It is the soul which contains our unique divine pattern for perfection in our use of the emotions, mind, and will. It is the soul which understands our unique needs for growth and redemption and our chosen pathway for progress and service in this life. The soul is our access point to the genuine experience of universal life; it filters and absorbs those aspects of divine intelligence, love, and will that we are capable of contacting and using. Through the soul, we can safely contact the universal and transcendent nature of God, without running the risk of being disconnected from our individual spiritual path.

5. The agent of spiritual integration in the personality is the higher mind. While the emotions can adore the life of spirit and the lower mind can theorize about its nature, the higher mind, when trained, can directly perceive and comprehend spirit. This comprehension is often quite limited, but as our use of our higher mental skills of intuition and discernment improves, the level of our comprehension does expand. This, in turn, enables the mind to direct the life and light of the soul intelligently into our subconscious patterns of thought and feeling—to repair, reform, heal, transform, and enlighten them. In this way, the trained and skillful mind, poised in the light of the soul, uses the act of meditation to direct the power of spiritual ideas and qualities into our memories, habit patterns, attitudes, and convictions, for the transformation of our character.

6. The actual work of meditation occurs mainly at the level of the unconscious and the deeper subconscious mind. The scope of the mind and spirit is far greater and more extensive than most people imagine—certainly far greater than the conscious mind can keep track of at any given moment. So most of the fruitful activity of a meditation will transpire at unconscious levels; the impressions we have at conscious levels represent only a portion of what is happening. This may be disappointing to those who judge the value and depth of meditations by the intensity of subjective impressions, but it actually makes good sense. Meditation is designed to lift our basic patterns of thought, feeling, and habit toward the light of the soul and its design for us. Since most of our patterns of thought, feeling, and habit are stored at subconscious and unconscious levels, it is natural that most of the work of meditative transformation will occur at these levels.

This does not mean that the conscious mind has no real role to play during a meditation; it is important that we remain alert at all times in meditation—receptive, responsive, and interested in what is happening. But we must strike a useful balance. A "meditation" in which the intellect seizes control and tries to run spirit through a rigid routine would be as disastrous as a passive and unstructured one in which the intellect falls asleep! The ideal is to strive for an enlightened cooperation between our conscious awareness and the design and qualities of the soul.

In other words, we should approach our meditations with a definite knowledge of the kind of help we need and expect, focusing our faith in the benevolent wisdom of spirit, our mind in the capacity of spirit to enlighten us, and our dedication in becoming more responsive to the direction of spirit. In this way, the conscious mind can summon and guide the energies of the soul to cleanse and reform the unconscious.

7. The only valid sign that a meditation has been effective is the permanent improvement of the quality of consciousness. Since meditation is a tool for the spiritualization of our consciousness and behavior, then the one sure sign that meditation is working is the gradual and steady enlightenment of our mind, character, and self-expression. Our values, priorities, and habits will become more responsive to spirit than the old forces of materialism. We will demonstrate more goodwill, generosity, and helpfulness in all that we think, feel, say, and do. We will understand more about the events and people in our life, and our confusion and inner conflict will be replaced by a dynamic state of clarity and peace. Old resentments and fears will drop away, old issues of guilt or self-pity will weaken, and we will have a much stronger capacity for self-acceptance. We will be inspired—and impelled—to get busy and resolve old conflicts, heal old prejudices, and become more active in using our talents to be helpful in the world.

And yet, as sensible as this yardstick of meditation is, many people use other measurements. They gauge the quality of meditation by how "deep" they go into trance or by how dopey and spaced out they become. In many circles, the number of symbols received or the clarity of visions experienced are held in great awe; in others, such superficial changes as smiling more and becoming quieter are accepted as proof of something marvelous. But greater blandness and dullness in outer behavior is not a step in the right direction for anyone except an aggressive psychopath, and they are not signs of effective meditation. Instead, they are signs that the personality is being systematically fragmented, destroyed, and devitalized—and a clue that a distorted form of meditation is being practiced.

All useful techniques and practices of meditation are based on these seven fundamental principles. Those techniques and practices which are at odds with these principles ought to be discarded. Those which were better suited for a simpler spiritual climate thousands of years ago ought to be consigned to the scrapbook—or at least thoroughly overhauled, so they once more serve a vital purpose. But those which help us discover the life of spirit, interact with its qualities and living forces, and integrate them into our conscious awareness, talents, and behavior should be seized upon and used as the tools with which we build a stronger bridge to the God within us:

The bridge which links heaven to earth in our own life.

Spiritual Breathing

The heart of an effective meditation is its ability to help us contact new elements of spirit, focus them in practical ways, and then direct them into our personality, transforming our character and self-expression so that we demonstrate the essence of the life of spirit in our daily living and work. In a sense, the act of meditation is something like "breathing" with the mind, except that we are breathing in spiritual force, not oxygen, and we are using our aspiration, faith, intelligent inquiry, and talents to do the breathing, not our lungs.

Physical breathing involves four phases: inhalation, a brief pause, exhalation, and a final pause. The act of meditation likewise is designed to involve four phases:

reorientation to the life of spirit, communion with spiritual forces, the integration of spirit into the personality, and contemplation—the grounding of the realizations and changes which have occurred in the first three stages in our awareness, habits, and activity.

It should be understood that the "breathing" of meditation has nothing to do with exercises which concentrate our attention on our physical breath, except to the degree that such exercises might be used *briefly* as a symbolic representation of the inner breathing which is about to transpire. The act of meditation is a dynamic activity of our intelligence, love, will, and talent—not a dull, mechanical process focused in our lungs, our spine, or anywhere else in the physical body. The scope of this dynamic activity will become clear as we examine each of these four phases of meditation in greater detail.

Reorientation. Most people are focused by habit in the needs, wants, worries, and activities of the personality. In order to meditate, they must therefore reorient the focus of their attention, withdrawing it from these needs and worries and activities and refocusing it in a conscious realization of the love, wisdom, peace, will, and joy of spirit. This is not done just by relaxing with a vague intent to contact spirit—or by tuning into some wonderful dream image of the heaven worlds. Building a bridge to spirit so we can commune with it means we must build this bridge, girder by girder, with the noblest elements of our intelligence, devotion, aspiration, and dedication. We must actually attune our consciousness—our capacity to know and understand—with the subtle forces of our spiritual self. As this attunement occurs, we must also then align the forms of our personality—our physical, emotional, and mental bodies—with the soul. Our goal in this initial phase of meditating is to transfer our attention toward a more refined level of consciousness while integrating the personality with spirit.

It must be understood that we are striving to make contact with *spirit*. Many meditators, unfortunately, never go any further than their own subconscious—especially those who, in a rush to reach heaven before the light goes out, make contact only with pleasant feelings and heavenly images. In most cases, they are only in contact with the "Mr. Goodfeel" department of the subconscious, a group mind, or one of the lower psychic planes.

Reorientation is achieved primarily through the intelligent use of our thoughts, emotions, and will, lifting ourself up to the level of spirit, so that the higher elements of our feelings, understanding, and motivation can interact with the spiritual forces of love, wisdom, and will. Not everyone is willing to do this—especially those who have accepted the distorted religious concept of self-rejection—but it actually makes good sense. The process of reaching out to summon and embrace our spiritual self is similar to getting to know a new neighbor. It would be silly to sit at home and wait for a new neighbor to come and knock on our door—and then respond to him with a blank stare, expecting him to do all the talking. It is just as silly to "sit at home" in our meditations, waiting for spirit to swoop down and lift us to heaven—and then expect it to "make us spiritual" without any effort or involvement of our own.

In meeting a new neighbor, we greet him with our friendliest mood, our most constructive thoughts, a generous hospitality, and a sincere offer to help. This is the way we should greet spirit in the reorientation phase of meditation as well. We should:

• Focus our attention on our *faith* in the value and benevolence of spirit and our *aspiration* to love spirit even as it loves us. In this way, we reach out to the presence of divine love, lifting our emotions up to the love of God.

• Focus our attention on *understanding* the design of spirit for our life and on our *trust* in the indwelling intelligence of divine life. In this way, we reach out to the presence of divine wisdom, lifting our mind up to the wisdom of God.

• Focus our attention on our *dedication* to learning more about spirit and our *commitment* to serve the purpose and power of spirit. In this way, we reach out to the presence of divine will, lifting our personal will up to the will of God.

Once we have attuned to these higher elements of thought, feeling, and will in this way, so they *become responsive* to spiritual direction, we are then ready to do the equivalent of "shaking hands" with our new neighbor, the higher self. This is done by registering this attunement in our subtle bodies of thought and feeling.

We register the new responsiveness of our faith and aspiration to spiritual love in the general area of our heart, and think of ourself as filled with the love of God.

We register the new responsiveness of our intelligence and trust in spiritual wisdom in the general area of our throat, and think of ourself as filled with the creative wisdom of God.

We register the new responsiveness of our personal will to spiritual will in the general area of our head, and think of ourself as filled with the purpose and power of God.

Should the act of registering our faith,

intelligence, and will in the heart, throat, or head produce unpleasant sensations of congestion or fullness, the unpleasantness can be diffused by refocusing our attention elsewhere.

When first beginning to meditate, careful attention should be given to learning each part of this phase of reorientation fully. It is easy to become sloppy and careless, but the price of carelessness is ineffective contact—or none at all. As we become proficient in our use of meditation, the time spent in this phase can be accelerated, but it should never be abandoned or skipped through by rote.

Obviously, the amount of time spent focusing our attention on our faith, intelligence, and dedication will vary with our individual needs. If we have extensive background in loving God, for example, the cultivation of faith and aspiration will be relatively easy. In this event, it will be necessary to spend more time reorienting our thoughts and will, so that we lift the whole of our consciousness to the level of spirit—not just one facet of ourself.

Some, of course, would be tempted to skip the reorientation of their thoughts and will, because it is difficult for them, and spend all their time in loving God, because it is easier. But this is a temptation we should resist. The life of spirit is balanced, and our approach to spirit should also be balanced. Otherwise, it will not be possible to invoke and live up to its design for us in the fullest sense.

We must also resist the temptation to go no further than this first phase of reorientation. To the beginner, the levels of tranquility, benevolence, and insight tapped during the phase of reorientation may seem so powerful that no additional effort is made. Yet very little enrichment of awareness, character, and behavior occurs during this initial step. To tap the full power of the tool of meditation, we must use the phase of reorientation only as an introduction, not a complete meditation.

Contact. In breathing, inhalation is followed by a brief pause in which the gases in the air we have inhaled mingle with the air already in our lungs. This interaction permits the oxygen to contact the delicate lining of the air sacs in our lungs, so it can be absorbed by our blood. In meditation, the first phase of reorientation must likewise be followed by a period of absorption or assimilation—a period of interacting with the power and life of spirit. This is the phase of contact.

Much of this contact occurs at unconscious levels of the mind, since the conscious mind is able only to glimpse or interact with a small portion of the full life of spirit. As a result, we may not be directly aware of the power we are tapping while we are actually meditating, and will only come to understand what has happened as revelations, insights, and healing qualities filter into our conscious awareness in the hours and days following our meditative contact. This does not mean, however, that we play no conscious role in the phase of contact. Quite the contrary, our conscious involvement is very important; by focusing on a specific need for wisdom, compassion, talent, strength, guidance, or some other spiritual quality, we give valuable definition and structure to our meditative contact.

It should be clearly understood that the purpose of this phase of contact is not just to reshuffle the old ideas and borrowed concepts of the unenlightened intellect. It is to interact with the quality of a particular divine force or ideal that we need for the enrichment of our character, thinking, and self-expression.

The activity of contact can be greatly facilitated by the intelligent use of a whole variety of meditative skills—the use of seed thoughts, affirmations, archetypal symbols, or mantras. We could use an affirmation from the Alice Bailey material, for example:

I am a point of light within the greater light of God.

I am a strand of love within the stream of love divine.

I am a point of sacrificial fire within the fiery will of God

As we sound this affirmation, we must dwell on what it means to identify with the greater light of God, the stream of love divine, and the fiery will of God. This is something greater than just loving these divine forces, or knowing they are there to help us; we become one with these forces to the best of our ability, learn about their nature, and tap their power.

Or, we may enter our meditation with an urgent need for greater forgiveness and tolerance in our daily life. We would therefore need to contact the force of divine forgiveness and tolerance—as well as our own spiritual design for expressing this force. To help us make this contact, we may find it useful to dwell on the seed thought "divine forgiveness" emanating as a gold light from a five-pointed blue star. The use of this archetypal symbol for divine love helps us fix a spiritual source of forgiveness in our own consciousness, thereby making it more readily accessible to us.

Perhaps our need is for guidance in solving some important questions or persistent problem. In this case, our aim should be to contact and interact with the wisdom of spirit. This can be accomplished by dwelling on a mantra such as:

The light of my soul pours through me as wisdom. I seek the light which illumines my path in life.

As we focus on these words, we should realize that they are a verbalization of a greater reality—the actual wisdom of the soul. We use the words to help us summon and interact with the essence of this wisdom and bring the abstract, formless light, love, and power of spirit into a level of understanding where we can register, comprehend, and utilize them. This is an active process which focuses our need to know and our commitment to grow, thereby producing a rich contact with spiritual wisdom.

These are but a few examples of the many techniques and tools that can be used to facilitate the work of contacting the life of spirit. If the purpose and activity of contact are comprehended, then almost any meditative technique can be skillfully used to produce this contact. But it must be understood that the goal of this phase of contact is not to produce a blinding or startling breakthrough. We contact and interact with spirit in order to enrich our consciousness. Genuine contact with spirit tends to be subtle and quiet—a steady uplifting of our perspective on life, not a blinding vision; a quiet acceptance of conditions which have irritated us in the past, not a cathartic change; a subtle registration of new confidence in what we are doing or a new appreciation of our opportunities, not an earthshaking revelation.

It can take some time to get accustomed to the quiet and subtle nature of genuine contact with spirit—especially if we have become addicted to sharp images, strong feelings, or high drama in our "meditations." But the interaction which produces sharp images and high drama is likely to be only a superficial brush with our subconscious desire for contact—not a legitimate registration of the life of spirit. So we must train ourself to recognize the hallmarks of genuine contact:

• A dawning awareness of the significance of what we do.
• A fuller recognition of our responsibilities.

- A greater ability to be at peace with ourself and the world.
- A new comprehension of our spiritual design.

Integration. Most of us think of exhalation as a time when stale air is expelled from the lungs, but it is also the time when new air, which has been absorbed into the blood, is "breathed" into the cells of the body to sustain vitality and metabolism. In meditation, much the same is meant to happen during the stage of integration. The new qualities and forces of spirit, which we have contacted and absorbed to some degree, must be worked into the fabric of our thought, feeling, and behavior, thereby integrating our spiritual self with our personality, enriching our character, and enhancing our self-expression.

To some extent, this integration occurs automatically in a meditative state, because genuine contact with the life of spirit will begin to affect unconscious patterns of thought, feeling, and behavior, even if we do nothing to help the process. But it should be obvious that integration will be far more effective if we *do* take a skillful hand in directing the modification of our character. It is relatively easy to experience new insights, serenity, goodwill, courage, joy, and compassion during "peak moments" of meditation, but not nearly so easy to bring these qualities and forces into our ordinary state of consciousness. The conscious intent to direct these spiritual energies into our subconscious storehouse of memories and behavioral patterns, to cleanse, heal, and enrich them, greatly facilitates the integrative process.

There are a number of simple ways to integrate the power and quality of spiritual force into the personality. One of the easiest is just to rest our intelligent attention and faith on the fact that our spiritual self understands and supports whatever is right, noble, just, and worthy of praise in our life. The good talents we are developing, the courage we are trying to muster, the joy we seek, the tolerance and self-discipline we are endeavoring to build, the knowledge we have gained, and the self-mastery we are trying to demonstrate are all noble elements of character which we can "hold up to the light of the soul," like a chalice, in the expectation that spirit will bless these developing character strengths and charge them with new life and force. The stronger our faith and expectation that spirit does support us in this way, the more powerful this exercise will be.

A second way of helping the work of integration is to charge up the strength of new realizations and states of consciousness we experience while meditating. If we suffer from excessive worry or fear in some area of our daily life, for instance, and experience a new level of detachment, confidence, and courage during a meditation, we can then focus our attention one-pointedly on these "new" states of detachment, confidence, and courage, magnifying them and charging them up. In this way, we strengthen our ability to act with these spiritual attitudes, even when we are not meditating.

As we gain expertise in meditating, it becomes possible to assist the work of integration even more directly, by focusing our awareness on an enlightened thought or quality and then reviewing those memories, attitudes, and values which are at odds with it. As we review these patterns of our own subconscious, we direct the healing love of this enlightened thought or quality into the heart of them, cleansing away the imperfection and revising these "bad seeds" so they become the good seeds of new and more spiritual behavior.

If we tend to be excessively grim in our approach to life, for example, we would focus our awareness on the joy of spirit. From this perspective, we would then review our ingrained habit of taking life too soberly. Without letting ourself be dragged into a new experience of grimness, we would examine each situation and see how we could have approached it with the joy of spirit instead of the pessimism of the personality. And we can actually direct the force of joy into these patterns to break them up and establish a new and healthier state of consciousness—a personality which is able to express cheerfulness and good humor, even when life is difficult.

This type of integrative activity is more difficult than the earlier examples, because it requires a well-developed capacity for detachment and self-discipline, the ability to consider the ideal and the actual conditions of some aspect of life simultaneously, and a strong and unwavering bond with our spiritual self. But these are all skills which ought to develop as we gain experience in the act of meditation. And as we apply these skills in this way, we vastly accelerate our ability to heal specific conflicts from the past and integrate the understanding and compassion of the soul into the regular thoughts and feelings of the personality. Instead of looking back in anger and frustration at our past, we can look back with love, understanding, and courage—just as spirit does. In this way, the structure of our character can be redeemed and cleansed.

The work of integrating the spiritual self with the personality never seems to end—because the scope of spirit is itself without end. Every time we enrich our character, this enrichment prepares us to rise to greater heights of awareness in subsequent meditations. Every time we learn to express more insight, love, strength, and joy in our daily behavior, the next level of insight, love, strength, and joy is opened to us, giving us something new and greater to integrate into our memories, behavior, talents, and concept of who we are. Little by little, our bond with spirit is strengthened in this dynamic but quiet process. Eventually, we reach the point where we are never without a sense of the presence of God in our midst—yet even then, there are greater measures of spirit to aspire to, undiscovered qualities and forces to integrate into our self-expression.

Through the work of integration, aspiration becomes realization. Good intentions become acts of goodwill. Courage becomes the strength of practical achievements. And the light of God is revealed within us and through our works.

Contemplation. The final stage of breathing, before we take our next breath, is a time when the oxygen, which has now reached the individual cells of the body, performs its ultimate function of sustaining and nourishing the intricate physiologic activities of the body. In meditation, the final stage is much the same. We have lifted our awareness up to the level of spirit, interacted with its qualities and forces, and integrated them into the patterns of our thought, feeling, and behavior. Now, we launch the work of grounding these new realizations and energies in our actual waking consciousness. This is the work of contemplation.

The term "contemplation" is often used to refer to vague and undirected speculations on the abstractions of life. But in its true sense, it refers to the ability to extract a practical application from an abstract force or quality. As we contemplate the realizations and experiences we have tapped during a meditation, we consider their practical and immediate application to our daily life. We devise specific values, convictions, attitudes, and plans which will help us express these new realizations in meaningful ways. And we focus our resolve to "complete the cycle" and shepherd these new ideas and realizations into physical reality.

If our meditation has led us to a deeper realization of tranquility and order, for example, the period of contemplation can be used to appreciate our own opportunities for expressing these qualities in daily life, as greater discipline, confidence, and organization. If we have tapped a new sense of purpose concerning our work, the period of contemplation can be used to translate this purpose into a more effective hierarchy of priorities, a clearer sense of our goal, and new ideas as to how best to proceed. If our meditation has filled us with a new measure of compassion and devotion to good, the time of contemplation can be used to appreciate more deeply the many ways we can act with greater goodwill and tolerance in our own life.

In a very real sense, meditation is like a trip to a first-rate museum or art gallery—not as a casual tourist, but as an avid student. As we move from one painting or display to the next, we are almost overloaded with insights, a deeper appreciation of beauty, and a more profound understanding of life. To properly appreciate the whole experience, we need to take time after we leave to sit down and digest the impressions of the day, before they escape us. So also, we need to digest the events of meditation—while still at a meditative level—before they get away from us. There are two reasons why this is important. The first is that the meditation has occurred at higher levels of consciousness than our ordinary waking state. If we do not take time to distil the insights we have gained, we may find it hard to remember what they were once we have left the meditative state. The second is the more meaningful: it gives us a chance to set a tone which will carry our meditative state into practical expression.

By examining the implications of our meditation, we can recognize more clearly the qualities and values we need to express as we interact with life and other people.

By recognizing areas in our character and behavior which need revision, we focus the impulse of personal growth.

By appreciating new possibilities in the events of life, we make it possible to see opportunities we have overlooked before.

In addition, we should dwell briefly on the fact that we have strengthened our bond with spirit; through the skillful and intelligent use of faith, trust, and dedication we have tapped a new measure of divine life. We have reinforced our conviction that spirit truly does love and understand us and is ready to help us. We have touched the wisdom of spirit, and this has enriched our understanding of life. We have touched the love of spirit, and this has enriched our capacity to be a force of goodwill. And we have touched the power of spirit, and this has enriched our confidence and ability to act in life.

Each successful meditation should help us understand more of what it means to be a spiritual person living in a somewhat imperfect body, personality, and world. By meditating, we deepen our understanding of what our spiritual design for perfection is—and we learn yet another lesson in how to manifest it more completely. So it is important to use the time of contemplation wisely, to enrich our comprehension of who we are, what our role in life is meant to be, and how we should play it out.

In this way, we enrich and transform not just our character, but also our self-expression—not by affecting the superficial appearance of sainthood, but by learning the practical lessons of translating divine love into individual goodwill, divine light into creative ideas, and divine will into constructive activity.

This brief description of the four phases of meditation should be viewed as a basic pattern for individual meditations, not a rigid formula to be followed without variance. As a pattern, it can be used by most people to improve the quality of their meditations, regardless of their temperament, potential, or place on the spiritual path. It is deliberately open-ended, so that adaptations can be made and new skills added.

In actual practice, the four phases will tend to overlap a great deal; a fresh insight may lead us to pause and contemplate its application right in the middle of a meditation, rather than wait until the end—just as we may start experiencing a substantial degree of contact with spirit while we are still only part way through the first phase of reorientation. The process of integration, in particular, may well occur during every phase of meditating—especially as we realize how much more peacefully and tolerantly we can think and feel toward outer circumstances, once we touch the healing goodwill of the higher self.

Still, even though overlapping will occur, it is important to maintain a sense of order and structure in our meditations. If we do not, we may find that the whole process begins to unravel, and our "meditation" becomes nothing but a passive withdrawal from the unpleasant realities of our daily problems and responsibilities. The sense of order and structure with which we direct our meditations need not be obtrusive, but it should be enough so that we always know what we are doing, why we are doing it, and what we hope to achieve. In this way, we can make sure that we are able to sustain a meaningful cooperation with our spiritual self, and not get off the track.

It is also important to understand that not every meditation will be bursting with exciting revelations or charged with love, peace, and joy. Just as we are not always able to speak or write as lucidly and as brilliantly as we do at peak moments of inspiration, our capacity to meditate effectively also varies. On some occasions, we will be so distracted that any effort requiring concentration is just too difficult. At other times, we will go through the paces of meditating, but nothing much will seem to happen. But these are often problems only of our conscious mind—not our spiritual self. By making the effort to meditate and focus our attention on the love, wisdom, and will of the soul, we set in motion at unconscious levels forces which enrich and expand our awareness. It is therefore valuable to set aside time each day to meditate and turn our awareness inward. If we do, then we will find that our meditative efforts are successful most of the time.

Above all, we must not try to make meditation into something it is not. Many people waste a great deal of time thinking that they must cultivate a deep and perfect capacity for concentration in order to meditate. This is not true. Only a light level of concentration is required—just enough to keep our interest focused in the light of the soul. When stray thoughts occur, we do not need to fight them or be disappointed by our "lack of concentration"—just let go of them and return to what we were doing.

Actually, a deep level of concentration can be a hindrance to good meditation, because the only way to achieve it is to militantly empty the mind. But this leads to an unfortunate state of passivity that makes true meditation all but impossible.

The act of meditation does not in any way suppress the personality. It teaches the personality to rise up to the level of spirit and breathe in the love, joy, peace, wisdom, and will to be found there. And having breathed, the personality is able to initiate a dynamic new cycle of life—a cycle of *spiritual* expression.

Our Great Challenge

We must always remember that meditation is a *tool* of spirit—a means to an end, and not the end itself. Like any tool, meditation can be used to build, repair, and reform, as necessary. The great value of meditation to spirit is that it can build, repair, and reform *consciousness*. If we keep this basic principle in mind, then our uses of meditation will likely be constructive and productive.

If we are careless in the way we use any tool, we can damage and destroy things— including the tool. Because meditation is a tool for building and repairing consciousness, the price we will pay for any failure to exercise reasonable common sense while using it may be quite high. Even though spirit is wise, we still need to use our own common sense and wisdom to cooperate with it successfully. Even though spirit is loving, we still need to learn how to translate this love into personal expressions of forgiveness, tolerance, and goodwill—not just use the power of the inner life to heighten our selfishness. Even though spirit behaves responsibly, we still need to act with a similar measure of responsibility as we meditate. If we do not, then we can be harmed by careless uses of this tool.

Those who use meditation just to passively suck on the life of spirit are not using this marvelous tool productively. They are like the farmer who was known far and wide as being the laziest farmer in the state. One day, a neighbor passing by saw that the farmer's hoe was broken.

"How did you break it?" the neighbor asked. "Hit a rock?"

"Nope," said the lazy farmer, "I leaned on it."

Just sitting in the stillness is *not* an effective use of meditation—it is the equivalent of leaning on the hoe. If we lean long enough, we will break the hoe. If we sit in the silence long enough, we will dull our mind, blunt our emotions, and bore the soul to the point where genuine meditation becomes almost impossible.

The proper use of meditation is to build within our awareness a strong and enduring capacity to interact directly with spirit. This cannot be done by leaning on our hoe! It is a great challenge—the greatest we face as a human being. And it involves many lessons, each of which teaches us yet another creative use for meditation. The most significant of these lessons are:

To discover the fullness of our spiritual nature. This is an endless task, because the more we discover, the more we find we need to revise our previous understanding. But despite the ravings of spiritual nihilists who claim it cannot be done—because they think only in absolutist terms—we *can* immensely enrich our understanding of our spiritual nature and its design for identity, thought, motive, attitude, and activity. We can strip away the outer layers which obscure our indwelling spiritual treasures and talents. We can learn through our own direct meditative experience that we truly are a part of the body of God, always surrounded by and a part of divine benevolence and power. And we can learn to respond to the presence of divine life in all things, not just ourself. Our individual grasp of these concepts may be partial and incomplete. *But we can know our spiritual nature and come to express it in our life!*

To bring the light of the soul to earth in and through our own activities. This lesson begins with the transformation of our character, as it has been described in this essay, and ends as we become a fitting agent for the light of the soul on earth. It is a slow process which unfolds step by step, as we evaluate ourself and our habits and then work to revise them. But with each step we take, we grow in goodwill and wisdom. And we begin to discover that we are not just working to transform our character to make us a better person. Our character is like a miniature laboratory in which we learn to work with divine force—to build new talents, to cultivate the treasures of spirit, to harness the impulse to grow, and to learn the basic lessons of creativity. Meditation is the tool which keeps the laboratory humming—a tool which can be a hundred times more powerful than modern psychology or hypnosis in modifying character and behavior, because it transcends our subconscious and unconscious and draws in the life of spirit.

Through this developmental work in the laboratory of our character, we gradually produce many wonderful things:
- A new sense of responsibility.
- A stronger capacity for leadership.
- Genuine creativity and genius.
- The talents we need to fulfill our spiritual design.
- A much larger capacity for compassion and goodwill.

To radiate this light of spirit to others and the whole of mankind As we become an effective agent of the soul on earth, we find the scope of our activity expanding as well as our consciousness. We become "a light on a hill," radiating the divine qualities of love, wisdom, and direction to the whole world and mankind. This opens up a new realm of spiritual service—the blessing of humanity and civilization.

The actual meditative work of radiating light and love to the world is very similar to the activities of our personal meditations. The only difference is that instead of sending the divine qualities of spirit to our subconscious, we send it to the whole of humanity. In other words, instead of resting in a conviction that goodwill, added to our attitudes, will solve many of our personal problems, we now dwell on the conviction that goodwill, expressed by men and women throughout the world, will enrich humanity's ability to cooperate with one another and solve its conflicts.

Indeed, the value of meditation as a tool of spirit is so great, and its uses so powerful, that it is really not a question as to whether or not a spiritual person should meditate. It is one of the duties of the spiritual person to make contact with the soul and use this contact to enrich life. It is therefore important to learn to meditate wisely and to use it as a basis for making our contribution to life.

Enlightened Cooperation

The act of meditation is primarily an act of discovery and activation—the discovery of our inner design for wholeness and the activation of its qualities and purposes in our own life. The discoveries we make in our meditations put to an end any doubt we may have about being only a physical being living in a physical universe, and introduce us to the real arena of life, the life of spirit. And the experience we gain while activating the forces and qualities of spirit in our own self-expression likewise puts to an end any doubt we may have about our own worth as a human being—or our worth to spirit.

If properly managed, the discovery of the inner dimensions of life does not produce in us any longing to escape the physical world; on the contrary, it inspires us to learn as much as we can about the laws, the patterns, and the qualities of spirit so we can then use them to make sense of and approach life in the physical plane more effectively. The more we meditate, the more we discover that some approaches to living—and meditating—are more effective than others. This helps us sharpen our skills in serving the life of spirit.

Eventually, we come to comprehend more fully the nature of spirit, the role of the enlightened personality, and the relation of spirit to the personality. As a result, we do not need to depend any longer on ancient teachings, no matter how valuable they may have been in the past. Through meditation, we have the means to investigate these issues ourself.

It is essential to understand that spirit has designed the personality to participate intelligently in this process of discovery and activation. The personality is meant to be directly involved in it—not just by passively adoring spirit, but by actually taking the lead in exploring the vast realms of consciousness. This exploration does require work—but the work is neither strenuous nor complex. It is the simple and pleasurable work of mining the treasures of spirit to be found within our own higher consciousness and integrating them into our own self-expression, so they can become the outlets of our spiritual will and service. Through these treasures, new spiritual life can enter the physical plane, to enrich our life and the lives of others.

Those who claim that the life of spirit is best approached by ignoring the personality—or worse, by trying to destroy it—soon find only the peace of impoverishment and emptiness. This simplifies life, but it does not enrich life. It does more to estrange us from the real life of spirit than draw us nearer. Without an effective personality, there can be no bridge between the realm of spirit and the physical plane—nor any means of demonstrating spiritual virtue and will on earth.

There is no question that the average personality often inhibits the life of spirit, just as poor soil prevents the vegetables and flowers we may plant in it from reaching their maximum yield. But no advantage is gained by getting rid of the soil altogether. The only way to genuinely improve the situation is to enrich the soil, so it can support a larger yield. The same common sense applies to the growth of the personality as well. If the soil is poor, it must be enriched.

Meditation, when correctly used, is a marvelous tool for enriching the personality—for preparing it so it can serve as a proper agent of spirit. As we develop our mental powers of discernment, analysis, creativity, and intuition, we enrich the mind's capacity to contact and comprehend spiritual wisdom. The enlightened mind then becomes an outlet for spiritual wisdom. As we develop and purify our emotional expression of devotion, aspiration, and reverence, we enrich our capacity to contact and use spiritual love. The compassionate heart then becomes an outlet for spiritual love. As we develop a more refined sense of purpose and the ability to act with courage and perseverance, we purify and strengthen the personal will, so it is in harmony with spiritual will. The enlightened will then becomes an outlet for divine will.

The achievement of this level of enlightenment requires *skill,* not just the willingness to love God. It requires skill that we can develop, refine, expand, and perfect. In fact, these are skills that only we can develop. God can give us wisdom, but we must still learn to use this wisdom to solve our problems. God can give us power, but we must still learn to use it constructively and wisely. And God can give us love, but we must still learn to use it intelligently and benevolently.

As our skill in meditating grows, we grow, too. Meditation complements our efforts to make our way in the world more effectively, more productively, and in greater harmony with our perfect design. As we accept responsibility for our own growth, the act of meditation helps us discover the path we are to tread—and the means for treading it. As we outgrow our habits of selfishness and learn to serve, meditation again helps us discover what it means to serve—and helps us develop the skills we need in order to do so wisely and constructively.

When we truly approach spirit with the intent to do what it would have us do, not what the personality wants, then we know our meditations have been effective. They have lifted us up to the highest level of human understanding, and we have stayed there, even while continuing to be involved in the life of the personality and the physical plane.

And when this has happened, then we have mastered another tool of spirit.

Ordering Additional Essays

Other essays being issued in Enthea Press gift editions include *Celebrating Life* ($7.95), *Working with Angels* ($7.95), *The Role Death Plays in Life* ($7.95), *Praying Effectively* ($7.95), and *The Way To Health* ($9.95.) They may be ordered by calling Enthea Press at 1-800-336-7769 or by sending a check plus $2 for shipping to Enthea Press, 289 S. Main St., #205, Alpharetta, GA 30201.

The rest of the essays are available only in their original form—as one of six essays in each volume of *The Art of Living* and *The Life of Spirit.* These books can be ordered for $8.95 each, plus $2 for shipping. The entire set of either *The Art of Living* or *The Life of Spirit* can be bought for $50 each, postpaid. These books can be ordered from Enthea Press as well.

Active Meditation: The Western Tradition, a more complete book on meditation by the same authors, is also available for $19.95 plus $3 postage.